10 Golden Money Tips

IN A WORLD OF GREEDY BANKERS AND VOLATILE MARKETS
What The Richest 1% Do With Their Money
That The Remaining 99% - Don't !

Published by MONEY-PORTAL
©2016 Jacob Nayman
All rights reserved.

The information within the "10 Golden Money Tips" is rooted in Nayman's extensive experience – distilling more than 15 years of expertise in his role as a leading investment adviser to the wealthiest.

The keys to achieving your financial goals and dreams are within your grasp

There are two major sources of financial opportunities - and dangers.

The first danger stems from the major financial institutions, such as banks and Wall Street: these companies pay their employees and executives high salaries and bonuses - with *your* money!

How does it work?

Their investment advice, for example, may be based on making you invest in what gives *them* (or their employers) the highest commission.

This means that the advice their financial "advisors" give you - most of the time - actually serves *their* needs - not yours.

The "10 Golden Money Tips" will give you the tools necessary to turn the tables and manage your finances to achieve your needs and desires.

The second danger is market volatility, which is expressed by inflation, deflation, fluctuations in interest rates, currencies and the stock market.

The "10 Golden Money Tips" will give you the ability to take steps to protect your money in times of uncertainty. You will learn how to use the volatility of the market as leverage to your advantage, to maximize your investments and earn a lot more money!

Equipped with the Tips in this book, you will know:

- How to create an income-generating asset from your savings.
- The most effective way to receive benefits from your bank.
- How to communicate effectively with advisors representing banks and investment companies - and as a result, you will be able to make optimal investment decisions that serve your needs only.
- How to identify the best mutual funds and ETFs.
- How to avoid buying exotic financial products - and why.
- How to obtain higher gains on your investments, with minimal risk.
- How to avoid the pitfalls set up by investment companies.
- How to pilot your money in changing market conditions.
- The investment habits of the richest 1%, which ones are right for you, and why you should adopt them.
- What the existing investment products are, and how you can use them to profit more with your money.
- What to demand from the financial experts managing your money, and how to get it.

Jacob Nayman's book "10 Golden Money Tips" reveals the financial practices used by the world's wealthiest. The information is rooted in Nayman's extensive experience – distilling more than 15 years of expertise in his role as a leading investment adviser to the rich.

The financial Tips outlined in the "10 Golden Money Tips" give you the optimal toolkit for the practical management of your financial investments, enabling you to maximize your profits in a world full of financial opportunities and dangers.

Buy the paperback edition of the "10 Golden Money Tips" and get its companion, "The 1%"
- for free!

Jacob Nayman's book

"The 1%"

reveals the financial practices used by the world's most affluent.

The combination of the

"10 Golden Money Tips"

and the money practices outlined in

"The 1%"

gives you the optimal toolkit for the practical management of your financial investments, enabling you to maximize your profits in a world full of financial opportunities and dangers.

LIMIT OF LIABILITY / DISCLAIMER OF WARRANTY

THE AUTHOR AND PUBLISHER HAVE USED THEIR BEST EFFORTS IN PREPARING THIS E-BOOK. THE AUTHOR AND PUBLISHER MAKE NO REPRESENTIONS OR WARRANTIES WITH RESPECT TO THE ACCURACY OR COMPLETNESS OF THIS E-BOOK AND SPECIFICALLY DISCLAIM ANY IMPLIED WARRANTIES MERCHANTABILITY OR FITNESS FOR A PARTICULAR PURPOSE. THE AUTHOR AND PUBLISHER ARE NOT ENGAGED IN RENDERING LEGAL, FINANCIAL, OR OTHER PROFESSIONAL ADVICE. IF YOU NEED LEGAL OR FINANCIAL ADVICE OR OTHER EXPERT ASSISTANCE IS REQUIRED, THE SERVICES OF A PROFESSIONAL SHOULD BE SOUGHT.

THE ACCURACY AND COMPLETENESS OF THE INFORMATION PROVIDED HEREIN AND THE OPINIONS STATED HEREIN ARE NOT GUARANTEED OR WARRANTED TO PRODUCE ANY PARTICULAR RESULTS, AND THE ADVICE AND STRATEGIES CONTAINED HEREIN MAY NOT BE SUITBLE FOR EVREY INDIVIDUAL. NEITHER THE AUTHOR NOR THE PUBLISHER SHALL BE LIABLE FOR ANY LOSS OF PROFIT OR ANY OTHER COMMERCIAL DAMAGES INCURRED FROM THE USE OR APPLICTION OF THE CONTENTS OF THIS E-BOOK, INCLUDING BUT NOT LIMITED TO, SPECIAL, INCIDENTAL, CONSEQUENTIAL, OR OTHER DAMAGES.

Table of Contents

The most effective way to receive benefits from your bank

Play it safe - diversify: get higher rewards with minimal risk

Golden Tip #6

Sometimes it's best to just "wait it out"

Golden Tip #7

"Pay to Play": the stock market's cover charge

Golden Tip #8

How to use mutual funds and ETFs as tools to manage your money

Golden Tip #9..........p. 47

How to avoid the 5 pitfalls of portfolio management

Golden Tip #10.........p. 54

Balancing your investment portfolio

Introduction

We live in an era of unprecedented technological change, a time of increasing life expectancy and a burgeoning culture of wealth.

Now, more than ever before, you as an individual should enjoy daily life while building the financial resources that will enable you to continue to enjoy life as you age. One of the most effective ways to achieve this goal is by taking a more active, informed role in the management of your personal finances.

During my employment as a senior investment adviser in the banking system, I accumulated thousands of hours of hands-on experience as I counseled clients from a wide breadth of sectors - high-tech, Ministry of Defense, wealthy clients, business owners, self-employed individuals, retirees and celebrities. What they all had in common was the desire to improve their money management and increase their profits. My experience with these individuals, combined with my subsequent experience as portfolio manager for the richest 1% of the population over the last fifteen years, is all laid out in the "10 Golden Money Tips."

Implementation of the tips and strategies that I reveal will give you the ability to both protect your investments and make much higher profits.

Yours,
Jacob Nayman

Golden Tip #1

The most effective way to receive benefits from your bank

Why are you and your bank at odds with each other?

Everyone wants to make a profit: individuals, small businesses, large businesses, banks, suppliers, and customers. Sometimes one person's financial gain is, necessarily, someone else's loss. From my personal experience as someone who's worked in the banking system, I know that the most important consideration for a bank is its profitability. Managers and employees are assessed and their performance evaluated based on this parameter. When they succeed in gaining higher profits, the result is larger bonuses for the employees themselves, as well as their superiors.

If you pay higher fees on your banking operations and receive a low interest rate on your savings, then the bank's profits will be higher. However, every additional dollar you earn (by negotiating with the bank for a higher interest rate on your savings and lower commissions) is a dollar that the bank is losing - the bank's profits are reduced.

Therefore, bank managers and employees have needs that are at odds with your own.

In a manner of speaking… you and your bank are at war.

IN MY EXPERIENCE

The parties that participate in a financial transaction do so only because they have something to gain. When you are equipped with the right knowledge and know to ask for benefits effectively, it puts you in a better negotiating position. The bank prefers to make a minimal profit on you than lose you altogether and earn nothing as a result.

When you do business with a specific branch for a long time, it seems obvious that friendships between you and some of the employees may develop. At this point, the bank clerk may be generous and give you good terms on your account, at their discretion. However, most banks have recognized the "problems" that may result from their employees favoring clients, and have sought to limit the benefits that the staff can offer.

Nowadays, receiving significant discounts or benefits requires the approval of a high-level representative. Consequently, even if you and the bank clerk are good friends - even soulmates, in the context of reducing commissions, it won't help much.

Effective ways to obtain benefits and reduce fees

Reduced fees for buying and selling securities
Reduced fees associated with managing one's bank account
Benefits of better interest rates on deposits

The ultimatum tactic

If you want to achieve significantly improved terms for your banking operations, the best thing you can do is tell the bank what you've been offered by a competitor bank.

You can't be vague: you must specify the name of the competing bank and the exact benefits or exemptions they've offered you - preferably noted by the competing bank in writing. The clerk at your bank will use this data to request similar terms for you: he will take the information you provide and send it to his managers for approval.

Along with your request for additional benefits, you can add the threat, either implicit or explicit, that if they can't meet their competitor's offer, then your money and income will be transferred to the other bank. Of course, if you are vague and have nothing to back up your threat/request, then your bank won't take you seriously.

Obtain benefits based on the status of friends or relatives

If you have friends or relatives who are considered preferred customers by your bank's local branch, you can ask them (if you are close) to request that the same benefits that they obtained for their bank account, such as high interest rates on deposits, low commissions on securities, and low account managing fees, be applied to yours. The idea is that the bank will see the total sum of the money across the various accounts and provide all accountholders with the same banking conditions.

Simulation: Using the ultimatum tactic

CLIENT: *"I want to deposit $50,000 into a savings account for a period of 10 years. What interest rate can I get?"*

CLERK: *"According to our official interest rates bulletin, you will receive an annual interest rate of 2%."*

CLIENT: *"A competing bank offered me 3.5%. I'd like to know if you can match that."*

CLERK: *"I don't think that such a high interest rate is going to be possible."*

CLIENT: *"Please inform the management that I will pull my $200,000 savings as well as my salary if I do not receive the interest rate offered by your competitor. Also, my father is a major client of* *yours; he expects that I, as his son, will receive the same privileges and conditions that he enjoys for his account – you can expect a visit from him in the next few days."*

Practical Conclusions

The bank operates as a business unit to maximize its profits. The bank's sole purpose is to make as high a profit as possible. When you, as a customer, receive one more dollar, whether from interest on your savings or as a result of reduced fees, the bank makes one dollar less.

The employees at the bank represent the interests of the bank, not yours. So if you're a passive customer, the bank will give you the default lower interest rate and charge you higher account fees. The bank will never equip you with the knowledge or the tools you need to get more than the absolute minimum.

If you find yourself in a situation in which the bank is trying to undermine your confidence, know that the negotiation tools presented here are already being routinely – and successfully – used by the bank's wealthiest clients.

Golden Tip #2

Play it safe – diversify:
get higher rewards with minimal risk

The relationship between reward/
return and risk

Why invest in something if you know that it's riskier? The only situation in which you should be willing to tolerate higher risk is one in which you expect to be rewarded with higher profits.

For example, take a racehorse: let's say that you decided to bet $1,000 on the horse "Lucky Star." His chances of winning the race are only 1 in 200, but if he does, the reward will be very high - you will profit close to $200,000. The only reason you would bet on "Lucky Star" would be if you knew, from the outset, that you would earn a great deal of money when he pulls off a surprising win.

Capital markets follow the same logic: the riskier the securities in which you invest, the more risk you take on, and the higher your chances of losing. At the same time, however, you increase the probability of gaining higher profits; if not, then there is no reason to take such a risk. If a higher risk doesn't carry the potential of a higher return, then naturally you should invest in something less risky.

IN MY EXPERIENCE

Suppose you have $200,000, and meet with an investment company that wants to manage your money. If they ask you, "How much do you want to earn?" your immediate, instinctive answer would probably be, "As much as I can!" But what are the implications of such a reply?

If, for example, you want to gain an average yearly return of 30%, then it's possible that you could actually lose 30%. Why? Because your investment portfolio will need to consist of securities with higher risk; for example, a greater number of shares relative to government bonds. If you want to gain only 10%, the possible loss will be adjusted accordingly: your investment portfolio will consist of many government bonds with a smaller exposure to stocks.

Practical conclusions of the risk vs. return relationship:

As an investor, it is crucial to understand the relationship between risk and return. Put simply, if you want more profit, you'll have to take more risk. Greater risk should only be taken if the potential return is high. If not, the risk should be avoided and the money placed in solid investments.

BE AWARE!

The total risk of a security is the sum of two types of risks:

1. Market risk

Market risk is the product of macroeconomic factors, such as a sharp rise in interest rates, inflation, deflation, a crisis in a major market player (Europe, the United States, or China), and more.

2. Specific security risk

Specific security risk derives from specific negative events such as strikes, mismanagement, embezzlement, or risk that decreases the company's profit due to an unexpected event. This type of risk may lead to a sharp drop in the price of the company's shares.

Why does diversity matter in risky securities?

Suppose you invest $300,000 in only one stock, and then the stock market goes up, while the one stock you invested your money into plunges. How can this happen? Here's one potential scenario: let's say that the CEO of the company you invested your money into is under suspicion of embezzlement. This is a "specific risk", i.e. a risk that is very specific to a certain security. In this example, because you didn't diversify your investment, you could stand to lose all of your money.

How to get higher returns with minimal risk

Research shows that a portfolio which contains over 20 different securities disables the specific risk element, making it irrelevant. The results of the studies performed also lead to another amazing and very important conclusion: if you invest in a small number of securities - 5, for example, and not at least 20 securities, you expose yourself to high risk **without** the reward of higher returns.

Practical Conclusions

There is a direct relationship between risk and return. If you want to increase your chances of higher profits, you have to increase your exposure to risk. "Don't put all your eggs in one basket" is the golden rule. If you violate this rule, you risk losing your investments with no higher probability of returns. Studies show that portfolio investment in at least 20 securities will achieve adequate diversification. In addition to, or instead of diversification, you can buy ETFs or mutual funds. By their very nature, ETFs and mutual funds are less risky because they spread their investment across many securities. However, it is important to remember that even if you eliminate the risk of specific dangers in your investment portfolio, you are still exposed to general market risk.

Golden Tip #3

Risk management as an instrument that protects our money

In the context of maintaining our standard of living, you can look at yourself as a "machine" that makes money. You usually wake up in the morning, brush your teeth, eat breakfast, and go to work. While at work you generate income that enables you to maintain the standard of living to which you are accustomed.

If the machine malfunctions - i.e., you get sick - two things happen: the "machine," in most cases, ceases to produce income; and your expenses increase due to the costs of your medical treatment.

BE AWARE!

Unfortunately, the government won't usually come to your aid. The combination of decreased income and increased expenses leads to a drastic decline in your standard of living. To avoid such a situation, you must build defenses that will offer you protection.

There are seven situations in which the "machine" will stop working: two are related to positive situations, and five are not. The positive situations include natural retirement from work or voluntary departure from the work place. The five negative situations include permanent loss of the ability to work; disease; disability; the need for long-term nursing care; and death. To protect yourself in case of one of these five negative situations, you must prepare a sufficient defense ahead of time, so that your standard of living, and that of your loved ones, won't be affected. For example, if you suffer a severe injury and are unable to work, lack of appropriate insurance coverage may leave your family financially unprotected. As a result, your standard of living can be severely impacted. Since the level of government aid is minimal, in some circumstances you may even find yourself at poverty level.

Why does insurance coverage actually protect your money?

Our defense system – also known as insurance - is our lifeline in situations in which our health is affected.

For example, if you need very expensive surgery, one that can only be performed abroad, or one that costs hundreds of thousands of dollars - a good health insurance plan will cover all of the expenses involved. Insurance, therefore, enables you to protect your health, and even your very life. In the situation above, what would you do without it?

The answer is simple: you would probably go broke. In an emergency situation, if you don't have an insurance policy to protect you and your loved ones, you'll likely be forced to use all of the money at your disposal, even taking out loans and spending your last savings, to fund the medical care necessary for survival.

However, when you have insurance protection, money **doesn't come out** of your pockets - instead, all of the costs are covered by the insurance company. The bottom line is this: the purpose of insurance coverage is to protect yourself from financial crises, and in some situations, even financial collapse.

IN MY EXPERIENCE

A wealthy acquaintance once complained to me that he pays rather high insurance premiums each month for individual insurance. I explained that these insurance policies basically defend his overall investments, and that if, heaven forbid, something would happen and he wouldn't have insurance coverage, he may have to sell one of his properties to cover his loss. Once he realized that the insurance is a tool for risk management, one that protects his financial investments as well as his assets, he felt much more at peace with his decision to pay the insurance premiums.

Practical Conclusions

From an economic perspective, insurance coverage can be considered a kind of financial policy. If you and/or your family members find yourselves in any type of negative situation (work disability, disease, disability, the need for long-term care or death) without the protection afforded by insurance coverage, the standard of living to which you are accustomed can be severely reduced, since *you* will be forced to bear the financial burden - and not the insurance company.

The general premise of insurance is that you, as a customer, are buying peace of mind – while the insurance company buys your risk.

When making decisions regarding your need for insurance coverage, it is important to consider five parameters:

1. What your needs are;
2. The coverage level provided;
3. The premium cost of the insurance coverage;
4. The quality of the company providing the coverage;
5. The professionalism of the insurance agent as well as the quality of service you receive.

From a holistic perspective, the protection afforded by insurance coverage can be considered a risk management tool. These particular tools protect our assets, financial and physical, accumulated over years of hard work.

Golden Tip #4

Make money, not percentages

It is better to earn 5% on a low-risk investment of $200,000 (a profit of $10,000) than to earn 30% on a risky investment of $5,000 (a profit of $1,500). Therefore, knowing how to invest in low-risk investments is important – often even more so than having detailed knowledge of speculative investments.

Why does the greatest profit come from the least risky investments?

Take, for example, an average investor (not a professional stock trader) who buys and sells securities on the stock market. This investor has $1,000,000 and decides to invest some of the money in oil and gas stocks, earning a 50% profit in three months. He invests the rest of the money in bonds, with which he gains only 6%. If this investor is like most people, he hates risk, so he will invest only $50,000 in oil and gas stocks and the remaining $950,000 in relatively low-risk securities. This strategy is appropriate, as the risk of stocks, particularly oil and gas stocks, is very high. After three months, he will have earned a 6% profit on the solid portion of his portfolio, totaling $57,000. This is more than his profit from oil shares, which amounts to only $25,000.

The less risky the investment, the more confidence you can have in allowing yourself to invest larger sums of money. Even if the percentage you earn is smaller than the percentage offered by speculative investments, the total sum of the profit will be significantly more.

BE AWARE!

The main difference between stocks and bonds is that in bonds, there is a guaranteed yield, if you hold the bonds until the end of their period. In stocks, however, there is no guaranteed yield.

Practical Conclusions

In the decision-making process, the least risky component of your portfolio is very important. Even if the percentage you get is smaller than the percentage offered by speculative investments, in most cases, the total profit from the solid part of your investments will be much larger than the profit from the risky part.

Golden Tip #5

How can you identify the best mutual funds?

What is the right way to choose the best mutual fund?

In order to understand the answer to this question, it's important for you to be familiar with a strategy called "all or nothing." Investment companies usually adopt this strategy in one of two scenarios. The first scenario is one in which a particular investment company is new to the market, and the majority of the public has not yet heard of them; they therefore have a greater motivation to stand out. The second scenario is when a large firm has problems with their customers: due to bad performance, their investors abandon the firm for their competitors.

IN MY EXPERIENCE

The general public is not aware of the subject of risk versus return. An ordinary investor is likely to say, "For me, the winning mutual fund this year is the one that gave the highest performance returns, because it earned the most compared to its competitors."

The basic idea behind the "all or nothing" strategy is to take significantly more risk than the competitors. If the company succeeds, it will win public appreciation, and the end result will be that more investors, having seen the "success" of the company, will buy its mutual funds. The investors are not aware that to achieve these "attractive" results, the company took big risks with their investors' money. If the company fails, on the other hand, their investors will suffer the damage.

The only way to protect yourself from the "all or nothing" strategy is to look at the company's long range performance. It's highly unlikely that an investment company that uses the "all or nothing" strategy will succeed, year after year, in achieving high returns.

BE AWARE!

In the seventies, investment company managers took their clients' money and invested it in very risky securities. If these securities succeeded, they would earn a lot of money; if not, they could lose it all. After making the investments, they took a plane and flew to Brazil.

Their plan was that if, after several weeks, the investment was successful, they'd return to the United States, where they would be received by their investors as financial geniuses. If the investment failed, they would stay in Brazil. Why Brazil? Because there was no extradition agreement in place between Brazil and the United States.

Practical Conclusions

Don't decide to invest your money in an investment company's mutual fund based purely on its short-term performance results. Base your decision on their performance over the last three to five years. In most cases, investment companies that show good results during this period of time are likely to hold their positive record in the future. If they don't, then of course act accordingly.

Golden Tip #6

Sometimes it's best to just "wait it out"

The confusion regarding the term "long-term investment"

When considering whether to invest in stocks or other risky securities, ask yourself whether or not you'll need the money in the short term.

For example, there is no sense in purchasing stocks if you know in advance that you'll need to use the money six months from now. The stock market can be extremely volatile: this means it's possible for the market to plunge during the six-month investment period, even though its relatively brief.

In this scenario, since you'd be forced to sell the stocks after six months, you wouldn't be able to stay for the long run and enjoy the possibility of market recovery. Practically speaking, your loss - because you can't keep your stocks for a longer period of time - becomes a permanent one.

If you know from the outset that you can't invest the money for a relatively extended period of time - at least two years - then it's better not to invest it in stocks at all. In the above scenario, if you could leave your money invested for a longer period, you'd have a better chance of recovering your loss, or maybe even making a nice profit as the result of a change in market trend. This latter example is an illustration of the term "long-term investment."

BE AWARE!

When the stock market weakens, or when there are indications that it will fall, there are many financial institutions that will try to encourage investors to stay in the market. Why? Because they profit from the commissions you pay them. Never just blindly follow their advice– make sure to analyze the situation and determine what is best for your finances.

Keep in mind, however, that the concept of "long-term investment," if not well understood, can have a negative impact on your financial decisions.

If you've already invested your money in stocks, it is definitely not recommended to hold the stocks for the long run no matter what. Suppose you invested your money and the stock market rises considerably. After a year, however, real economic concerns develop that the stock exchange will fall in the near future. In this scenario it is better to take action - ensure that you are less exposed to stocks, or in extreme cases, withdraw all of your money from the stock market. In this way, you can protect your financial investments and safeguard the profits you made so far. In this scenario, keeping your "long term investment" would cause financial damage.

Practical Conclusions

If you know that you can't leave your money invested for at least 2 years, then it is better not to invest it in stocks at all. In bad economic times, don't just passively leave your money invested for the long term. In some situations, it's a good idea to withdraw some or all of your investments to safeguard against significant future losses; in other situations, it's better to "wait it out " until better days come.

Golden Tip #7

"Pay to Play": the stock market's cover charge

We all know that we should buy stocks at a "cheap" price and sell them at a "high" price. The problem is identifying the two points at the ends of the spectrum - the minimum and the maximum value of the stock.

In practice, there is no guaranteed method to pinpoint when it is optimal to buy or to sell stocks. One way to estimate the best time to buy or sell is to rely on speculation based on futuristic economic analysis of the stock market. Another way is to wait for the market to "speak" - to show signs of life. In this method, you purchase stocks only after the market shows larger trading volumes and positive macroeconomic data. However, because you wait for the market to "speak," you are still in "standby" when the market begins to rise; therefore, the prices of the stocks you purchase will be higher. The difference between the price you could have paid for the stocks at the start of the rise and the higher price you pay later is the cover charge - the "entry premium". This "entry premium" is worth its cost, because by waiting, you invest your money in a market that shows concrete signs that the timing of your investment is right.

Practical Conclusions

Sometimes, it makes more sense to wait before investing in stocks. If you buy at a higher price and in a positive stock market environment, then in most cases, the entry premium will be worth its price.

Golden Tip #8

How to use mutual funds and ETFs as tools to manage your money

Mutual funds are one of the main instruments for investment in securities. They cover a wide spectrum of risk levels and returns, and can therefore satisfy a wide range of customer needs.

How do mutual funds work?

Mutual funds pool money from many investors to purchase securities, which include stocks, bonds, money market instruments and similar assets. In essence, mutual funds are joint investments. When you invest your money in them, they allow you to use licensed portfolio managers to manage your investment and thereby benefit from their knowledge and experience.

Mutual funds can represent a satisfactory solution for your needs as an investor, and compose an integral part of your private investment portfolio.

IN MY EXPERIENCE

It is important to note that even if you invest only a thousand dollars in a mutual fund, you will enjoy the same return as other investors who have invested larger sums in the fund, for example, over a million dollars.

The benefits of investing through mutual funds:

☗ Professional management

Mutual funds are managed by portfolio managers - skilled professionals who have extensive knowledge of the capital market and securities. The portfolio manager takes into account all of the conditions and factors that affect the stock exchange:. he monitors industry and economic trends, searches for the right company in which to invest the portfolio's capital and determines the appropriate time to do so, and makes decisions regarding asset allocation.

☗ Investment diversification

Mutual funds adopt the golden rule - "don't put all your eggs in one basket." Thanks to their diversification, you can get maximum returns with minimum risk.

☗ Liquidity

Mutual funds are bought and sold on the market every day, meaning that you can sell yours whenever you like.

☗ Transparency

The mutual fund is required by law to publish a prospectus before beginning its operations. A prospectus is a document that contains important details for investors deliberating whether to join the fund, such as specifics regarding investment policies and the like.

BE AWARE!

Alongside the advantages mentioned so far, there are also disadvantages – the most significant of which is the management fee, which is sometimes unduly high.

The disadvantages of using mutual funds

The question arises as to whether the fees for active management charged by the portfolio managers - the main cost of investing in mutual funds - are justified. The answer is that the fees are justified only if the annual returns you get on the fund, after payment of the fees, are higher than the returns you would have gained if you had bought an ETF (exchange traded fund), minus its cost. In many cases, ETFs that mimic indexes, like the S&P 500 index, give higher returns than mutual funds.

An ETF is a marketable security that tracks an index, commodity, bonds or a basket of assets. Unlike mutual funds, an ETF trades like a common stock on the stock exchange. The price of ETFs changes throughout the day as they are bought and sold on the stock exchange.

IN MY EXPERIENCE

ETFs are similar to mutual funds in several ways. Like a mutual fund, an ETF is a pool of investments. However, an ETF will often have lower associated costs than a similar mutual fund. Mutual funds have been a popular way to invest for several decades, whereas ETFs are relatively new. The popularity of ETFs is based on three factors: lower cost, better tax treatment and their returns compared to mutual funds.

Personal portfolio management through mutual funds and ETFs

As an investor who manages their own personal investment portfolio, you should decide during which periods of time to invest in mutual funds/ETFs. You can think of mutual funds or ETFs like a train running along the market's trend line (i.e. the "tracks"). You, the investor in these funds/ETFs, are not the train driver, but a passenger who can choose when stay on the train and when to get off; in addition to buying and selling, you can also decide how much money to invest. The yield of the funds/ETFs is not necessarily equal to your return: your return will depend only on your financial decisions, which determine the timing and the amount of your investment.

If you think the market is doing well, increase your exposure to risky assets by purchasing riskier funds/ETFs. When you see that the market is coming close to peaking and is saturated, you can decide to minimize your exposure to risk by moving your money to less risky investments, namely solid mutual funds or ETFs. When the stock market is doing poorly, maintain liquidity in the solid (low-risk) channel.

If you think the market is at the end of its period of recession and you have the opportunity to buy securities at low prices, then increase your exposure to risky securities. How? You can do this by transferring some of your money from the solid funds/ETFs to more aggressive funds/ETFs. Don't try for high accuracy in timing, such as purchasing securities at a low price and selling them at a high price: these attempts will likely result in financial damage. Instead, focus on managing your exposure to stocks/risk according to your personal preferences and the changing market conditions. If necessary, "wait it out" until better times come.

Practical Conclusions

Think of mutual funds or ETFs as tools that can be used for managing your money. Although they are actively managed by professionals, it is your responsibility to make the financial decisions that will enable you to maximize your profits.

Golden Tip #9

How to avoid the 5 pitfalls of portfolio management

What is a portfolio manager?

Portfolio managers are licensed financial professionals. Their license allows them to manage securities and to make investment decisions using money that other people or companies have placed under their control.

The main objective of the portfolio manager is to ensure that the investment objectives of their investors are met. The manager balances risk against performance in an attempt to maximize returns at a given investor's risk preferences.

48

IN MY EXPERIENCE

You and the portfolio manager have a common interest, which is first and foremost to achieve a high return at a given risk preference. The reason for the shared interest is that the portfolio managers know that if they do not produce lasting results to your satisfaction, you will take your investments elsewhere.

5 Pitfalls You Must Avoid at All Costs

 ## Pitfall #1

In all of the cases in which investors were robbed of their money, their biggest mistake was their decision to transfer money to an account not registered in their name, but in the name of a person who promised them large returns without risk. If a licensed portfolio manager wants to manage your money, he should do so from an account that is in your name only.

What should you do?

Open an account that is in your name only

You, as a customer, can decide by which institution your portfolio will be managed. The institution you choose will open an account in your name.

 Pitfall #2

If a portfolio manager doesn't "bother" you with a lot of questions - only promises that you will get a high return on your money, without any risk, then your money is in great danger. This behavior is a strong indication that you are not dealing with a professional portfolio manager - or worse, that they are most likely a con artist.

What should the process of opening an investment account be like?

Customization of the portfolio to your needs

We can compare portfolio management to a tailor sewing a suit. After an in-depth conversation with you, his customer, the portfolio manager can match the composition of the assets held in your investment portfolio precisely to your requirements: financial needs, financial goals, and returns vs. risk levels, as per your character/personal preferences.

Pitfall #3

If the investment company enjoys fees from the commissions of purchase and the sale of the securities, then the additional fees you pay should be minimal and the number of selling and buying operations should be reasonable. If this is not the case, then the cost of operating your portfolio will be so high that your odds of making a profit will be low. The only one who will profit from your portfolio will be the investment company.

What should you expect?

You should pay low commissions/fees

Management fees are the main fees that you, as a customer, must pay the portfolio manager for his services. The costs depend on the size of your portfolio: the larger your portfolio, the lower the costs per year (in percentages).

Pitfall #4

In some cases, the portfolio manager may not have enough experience, and because he wants to get results "no matter what the price" he may choose to take unnecessary risks, endangering your money. It's a bit like choosing a doctor - find one that has an extensive experience and a good record.

How should your portfolio be managed?

Your portfolio should be adapted to changing market conditions

A portfolio manager's objective is to maximize your profits at a given risk level. The portfolio manager should take all of the conditions and factors that affect the stock exchange into account. He has to monitor industry and economic trends, search for the right company in which to invest the portfolio's capital and determine the appropriate time to do so, and make decisions regarding asset allocation.

 Pitfall #5

There are some investment companies whose only goal is to gain large profits from the commissions paid by their clients; that way the workers and managers can enjoy high salaries and big bonuses. Their largest commissions come from their top customers, so in most cases they will do almost anything to retain them as customers.

The fear that their preferred customers will be dissatisfied with their returns and turn to other investment alternatives sometimes leads big investment firms to a breach of ethics.

Here's an example: suppose that a big firm considers their top customers to be those that have investments over $5 million. To increase the returns of their top customers, they do the following: first, they invest in securities for their top clients, and after that, they buy those same securities for their other clients. As a result of this strategy, a sudden high demand for these securities is created in the market, which leads to a dramatic price increase. The firms then sell the securities of their top clients at a considerable profit while ignoring their other clients. With this kind of strategy, the "success," or profit of the top clients is at the expense of the "little" customers. This form of unethical activity is, not surprisingly, considered a criminal activity. Numerous investments firms - many of them large and prestigious – have been caught performing this sort of manipulation and found guilty of fraud in a court of law. In most cases they got away with it by paying large fines.

How can you protect yourself?

One of the best ways to protect yourself from such companies is to do an online background check before you invest with them - simple internet research to see if their names come up, .

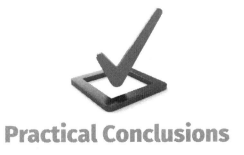

Practical Conclusions

When running your investment portfolio, you can invest in mutual funds or ETFs. The decision in which mutual funds or ETFs to invest and how much money to put in each channel - is yours. If after a while market conditions change, you are also responsible for making the decision to sell the mutual funds or ETFs and switch to others that are more suited to the new conditions created. However, if some or all of your money is managed by a portfolio manager, you as a client can rely on their expertise. You have to assume that his decisions are based on professional considerations.

The responsibility of the portfolio manager is to navigate your portfolio according to your needs and the changing market conditions and to maximize your profit. If after a while you see that this is not the case - don't stay with them! For example, if after 2 years you note that the returns on the risky part of your portfolio are less than the returns on the S&P 500 index for the same period of time, you can conclude that the explanation is that your portfolio has fallen prey to pitfall #2, #3, #4 or #5 - or a combination of them. If this happens to you, don't delay: it's time to move on.

Golden Tip #10

Balancing your investment portfolio

When you are building a private investment portfolio, one of the most important decisions is its division into two parts: the riskier part, from which you can gain a higher return and the less risky, or "solid" part. Depending on the dynamics of the stock market, it may be necessary to adjust the ratio between the risky and solid parts of your portfolio.

For example, due to an increase in the stock market, the most dangerous part of the portfolio may have risen to 50% - instead of the 20% you intended when you were first building your investment portfolio. What should you do in this scenario to balance your portfolio?

IN MY EXPERIENCE

When you have a managed portfolio, the investment company does the balancing for you.

The process of balancing your portfolio

Balancing your portfolio means buying and selling securities in a way that will return the portfolio to its desired risk levels. They do not have to be the same risk levels you chose when you first built the portfolio.

Decisions related to changing the proportions of the risky/solid portions of your portfolio should be based on present macro-economic data and your own, personal risk preferences.

Keep in mind that if you gain relatively large returns on your portfolio, you might prefer to have greater exposure to stocks. You may be able to take more risk since after all, even if the market were to drop, you would probably only lose money you already earned as a profit (and not your original investment sum). And of course, always remember that greater risk can lead to higher profits.

Practical Conclusions

Check your investment portfolio every 3 months to see if the proportion of risky vs. solid investments is appropriate. If necessary, balance it according to your risk preference.

Epilogue

REMEMBER:

**You won't get any prizes just for knowing things
you'll only be rewarded for your actions.
You gained valuable information:
Use it!**

Has this book helped you better understand
and manage your finances?
Please let me know - post an Amazon review.
Much appreciated,
Jacob Nayman

What next?

Enjoyed reading the "10 golden money tips"?

Have you already read "The 1%"?

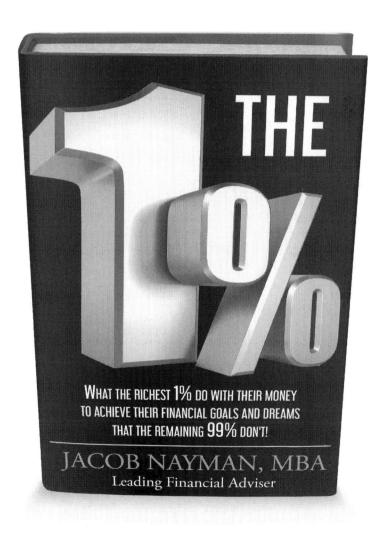

Jacob Nayman's book

"The 1%"

reveals the financial practices used by the world's most affluent.

The information within is rooted in Nayman's extensive experience – distilling more than 15 years of expertise in his role as a leading investment adviser to the wealthiest.

The combination of the

"10 Golden Money Tips"

and the money practices outlined in

"The 1%"

gives you the optimal toolkit for the practical management of your financial investments, enabling you to maximize your profits in a world full of financial opportunities and dangers.

THE 1%

WHAT THE RICHEST 1% DO WITH THEIR MONEY TO ACHIEVE THEIR FINANCIAL GOALS AND DREAMS THAT THE REMAINING 99% DON'T!

JACOB NAYMAN, MBA
Leading Financial Adviser

The 1%

What The Richest 1% Do With Their Money
To Achieve Their Financial Goals and Dreams
That The Remaining 99% Don't!

© 2017 Jacob Nayman
All rights reserved.

The practices within *"The 1%"* are rooted in Nayman's extensive experience – distilling more than 15 years of expertise in his role as a leading investment advisor to the wealthiest.

Do you want to create an income-generating asset?

In a world, of greedy bankers and volatile markets, learn how to gain significantly more profits with your money and enjoy financial freedom.

There are all sorts of ways to live and retire financially secure. One of the more practical methods is to use your savings as a base for the construction of a private investment portfolio that generates additional revenues. These revenues will give you the ability to maintain a high standard of living that suits your present and future needs.

Jacob Nayman's book "The 1%" reveals the financial practices that the wealthiest use. The money practices outlined in "The 1%" give you the optimal toolkit for the practical management of your financial investments, enabling you to maximize your profits in a world full of financial opportunities and dangers.

Table of Contents

Creating an income-generating asset

BENCHMARKING

PMaking optimal investment decisions

The 3rd practice of the 1%...........p. 83

Creating an optimal financial environment

The 4th practice of the 1%...........p. 92

Using core-satellite asset allocation strategy

The 5th practice of the 1%...........p. 99

Building your risky investments as an independent entity

The 6th practice of the 1%..........p. 106

Building your solid investments as an independent entity

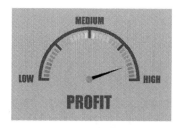

The 7th practice of the 1%..........p. 114

Choosing the best funds and ETFs

The 8th practice of the 1%..........p. 122

Profiting from the expertise of financial institutions

The 9th practice of the 1%..........p. 129

Avoiding exotic financial products

The 10th practice of the 1%..........p. 138

Understanding leading market indicators

Introduction

Having a good income is not always enough to secure your economic future: for that, you also have to acquire an asset / investment portfolio that generates additional income. There are all sorts of ways to live and retire financially secure. One of the more practical methods is to use your savings as a base for the construction of a private investment portfolio that generates additional revenue. This revenue will give you the ability to maintain a high standard of living that suits your present and future needs.

"The 1%" reveals the financial practices that the wealthiest use. Its practices are rooted in Nayman's extensive experience – distilling more than 15 years of expertise in his role as a leading investment advisor to the rich".

The money practices outlined in "The 1%" gives you the optimal toolkit for the practical management of your financial investments, enabling you to maximize your profits in a world full of financial opportunities and dangers.

Yours,
Jacob Nayman

The 1st practice of the 1%

Creating an income-generating investment portfolio

How much money do you need in order to feel financially secure?

Most people reply that they need $100,000 a year or more. If you take a couple in their 30's that has 3 children, it certainly makes sense. Assuming that the average life expectancy is 90 years (according to current predictions for the 21st century), a simple calculation shows that this couple will need an aggregate amount of $6,000,000 in order to maintain a reasonable standard of living over the next 60 years.

This illustrates the existential need to create an additional source of income for protection, to allow us to maintain a reasonable standard of living in the future.

One practical way to generate additional income is to manage our finances in an optimal manner. We can do this by creating and managing a private investment portfolio.

There are six ways to make sure you are financially secure

There are several ways to become financially protected:

1. Option one is to marry a rich spouse. However, experience shows that this transaction often comes as a package deal with unwanted extras - so it could prove less attractive.

2. A second possibility is to inherit money from your parents. This is not under your control, and even if you are lucky enough to inherit a large sum of money, you have to know how manage it wisely.

3. A third option is to be promoted to a very senior position at one of the largest private monopolies.

4. Option four is to reach a senior position at a company or other framework with public sector wages and very high pensions.
   Of course, the chances of promotion to such senior positions are small, and there are a limited number of such opportunities - to achieve option 3 or 4, you'd have to overcome many obstacles.

5. The fifth option is to establish your own start-up based on a clever and original idea, form a team of quality people, work hard, enjoy a suitable business environment and build a successful business based on your talent. Examples of such successes are relatively few. Statistics show that most entrepreneurs fail, and that the rest stagnate for years with no significant gain in capital.

Many of the "success" stories have a veiled explanation for their success. Often, the secret of "success" of such an entrepreneurship is shady: for example, the entrepreneur has connections with a public entity - a government institution, or a public corporation.

Unfortunately, for most of us, none of the first five options mentioned are relevant. Moreover, even if we belong or will belong to these categories in the future, it is important that we learn to manage our money wisely. In my experience, clients for whom one or more of the first five options are relevant learn how to optimally manage their money.

6. The final option, option 6, is to acquire in-depth knowledge and understanding of how to manage a private investment portfolio. Why invest your savings in a portfolio? Because in order to maintain a reasonable standard of living over time, you need to generate a satisfactory income stream. An investment portfolio, properly managed, will enable you to generate additional revenues of thousands of dollars and more each year from your savings. This sixth option is the subject of this book.

If, for example, you as an investor invest all of your money in a bank deposit with a fixed interest rate, your savings will likely be impacted if the CPI (consumer price index) suddenly rises - the damage will be expressed in reduced purchasing power of your money. So even if you consider yourself a conservative investor, it is important to remain vigilant and to change your investment channel from time to time, depending on market conditions.

The relationship between income, wealth, and an income-generating asset

Years of experience in the financial system have shown me that although there are many people who make a good living - sometimes over $200,000 a year, many of them don't make any effort to save money - they spend it all. It is important to understand that wealth is not defined as your income level. If your yearly income is high, but you spend it all, then you're just keeping up a high standard of living - for now. Wealth is defined by what you save, not what you spend.

In this book, we will focus on how to increase your revenue stream.

One way of increasing your revenue stream is by using your savings as a capital base for an income-generating asset. An income-generating asset can be a second apartment that you own and lease, which generates an ongoing revenue stream; or, alternatively, a sum of money invested in an investment portfolio that returns a profit. When you don't have an income-generating asset, your income is completely dependent on how many hours you work: the more you work, the more you earn. If you do not work at all, you will not have any income (other than social welfare payments). Creating / building an income-generating asset (such as an investment portfolio) allows you to produce a constant revenue stream even if you do not work at all.

IN MY EXPERIENCE

There are two types of investors: those who generate additional income by managing their private investment /savings portfolio and those who generate additional revenues by buying homes and offices and leasing them for rent.

It is important to note that today you can very easily enjoy benefits equal to those obtained by buying and leasing properties from private investment portfolios. By buying ETFs and mutual funds specializing in real estate investments, you can enjoy the same benefits from your investment portfolio as an investor who buys real assets directly.

Practical Conclusions

Having a good income is not always enough to secure your economic future: for that, you also have to acquire an asset / investment portfolio that generates additional income. There are all sorts of alternatives to live and retire financially secure. One of the practical methods is to use your savings as a base to construct a private investment portfolio that generates additional revenues. Those revenues will give you the ability to maintain a standard of living that suits your present and future needs.

The 2nd practice of the 1%

Making optimal investment decisions using financial tools

BENCHMARKING

When you manage your own private investment portfolio, there are times you have to make important investment decisions. In such situations, you may get misleading information designed to tempt you into buying a financial product that doesn't necessarily suit your needs. Such information can be given to you via different channels: the bank system, an investment company, or one of the media channels (financial newspapers; radio, television, or the internet).

You should consider this information carefully: the motivation to sell you the product may be the profit to be gained from the commission if you are persuaded to buy it.

This type of situation raises the question: what tools are available to you, as an investor, to help you make decisions that best serve your financial portfolio?

There are two powerful tools used frequently by the top percentile: **the benchmark standard** and **the Sharpe ratio - risk vs. return**

We can enjoy using powerful tools - the benchmark and the Sharp index - to simply, easily and effectively manage our private investment portfolio without knowing the mathematics or statistics behind these tools.

BE AWARE!

When we drive a car, we can enjoy the ride and arrive quickly and safely at our destination even if we have no knowledge or understanding of the car's mechanics. The same logic applies to financial instruments that help us make better financial decisions.

When should you use these tools?

These tools should be used whenever you are considering investing in a new financial product and when you need to decide whether or not to replace a product you already own.

The benchmark standard

What is a benchmark?

A benchmark is a standard against which the performance of a mutual fund or the performance of an investment manager can be measured. When evaluating the performance of any investment, it's important to compare it against an appropriate benchmark. For example, if one of your investments is in a mutual securities fund in Europe, you should compare it to an index that consists of European securities.

To evaluate the performance of your investment manager or your private investment portfolio you can use the S&P 500, the Dow Jones Industrial Average, or the Russell 2000 Index.

If you want to buy or evaluate an existing mutual fund you should use the Lipper indexes, which are based on the 30 largest mutual funds in each specific category; if you are also considering investing some of your money in international markets you should use the MSCI Indexes as your benchmark.

The investment managers know that their performance (in portfolio management or mutual funds) is judged by benchmarks, so they have an incentive to beat them. However, if they do beat their benchmark, you, as an investor, should ask yourself what "price" you're paying for the excess profit that you receive. While it may be that your investment manager simply has the professional abilities and skills that enable them to beat the market, the secret of their "success" may be substantial risks taken that put all of your investments in danger.

How to use the benchmark in the right way

Always check what happened to mutual fund returns over a minimum period of three years. Examining a period of at least 3 years reduces the likelihood that the results are based on a combination of luck and high risk taken by the investment manager and are not the result of professional investment managing. Even if the company is in fact taking unnecessary risks, it is much less likely that they're succeeding, year after year, while taking *significant* risks. For this reason, the average profit over three years can certainly indicate the level of professionalism of the investment manager

It is important to note that you should compare not only to the benchmark but also to other financial products with similar compositions, e.g. other, similar funds.

The Sharpe ratio

Risk vs. return

This ratio is another powerful tool that gives us more confidence in our financial decisions. It answers the question of whether or not the "secret" of success of an investment manager lies in higher risks taken with our money at our expense. Using the Sharpe ratio will protect our investments from such financial dangers.

What is the Sharpe ratio?

The Sharpe ratio is a tool for the calculation of risk-adjusted return. The Sharpe ratio can help explain whether a portfolio or investment company that has returns in excess of the benchmark is backed by smart investment decisions (made by the investment manager) or is the result of taking too much risk. A higher Sharpe ratio indicates better performance of the investment manager or mutual fund.

For example, suppose you have 2 investments that gave an average 10% profit per year over the last 3 years, but one investment (investment A) does so with half the risk of the other (investment B). In this scenario, you will obviously choose to invest your money in investment A - the one with the same return but less risk.

Now, consider another scenario: investment A gives you 20% per year and investment B gives you 10% per year, but investment A has 3 times the risk that investment B has. In this confusing situation, which investment should you choose?

Simple! Check the given Sharpe ratios of the two investments. The investment with the higher ratio is the preferred investment. If a portfolio or fund has higher returns than its peers, it is only a good investment if the Sharpe ratio is also the same or higher; if this is not the case, then those higher returns come with an additional, unjustified risk. In such a case, you should consider choosing a different fund with a higher Sharpe ratio.

NOTE: You do not have to calculate the Sharpe ratio - it is calculated for you in advance.

Simulation: Effective communication with an investment consultant

Investor: *"I want to invest $10,000 in a mutual fund that specializes in the field of real estate assets."*

Consultant: *"We have one that performed very well last year."*

Investor: *"Please give me the Sharpe ratio results for the 10 best funds from the last 5 years. Funds that specializes in real estate assets, of course".*

Consultant: *"Here is the list you requested, with the returns and Sharpe ratios".*

Investor: *"I see the top two have the highest returns as well as higher Sharpe ratios. I'd like to buy them at $5,000 each".*

NOTE: The information provided by the consultant can easily be found online.

IN MY EXPERIENCE

I remember a hedge fund manager, a specialist in biotechnology funds, who stated in the media that he employed eight researchers with PhD degrees to study the biotechnology market, as well as a professor who won the Nobel Prize. But a very simple test showed that the performance of his hedge fund compared to other, similar funds in the past 3 years - including the benchmark - was not very impressive.

What's the message? When you use, the right tools to make financial decisions nobody can confuse you.

Practical Conclusions

When you need to make the decision whether to buy a financial product or keep a product in your private investment portfolio, it is recommended to use at least one of the following tools: the benchmark or the Sharpe index.

Using these simple but powerful tools will protect you from purchasing inferior financial products and allow you to enjoy the best investment managers.

The 3rd practice of the 1%

Create the optimal environment for your investment portfolio

Your private portfolio can be managed via several platforms: a bank, an investment company, or a brokerage firm.

When you have an account set up to manage your private investment portfolio, the activities in this account will naturally be financial in nature, e.g. buying and selling stock market securities or financial products. Your main goal should be to make investments that are profitable for you - it's safe to assume that you wouldn't want your financial activities to satisfy or benefit only the needs of the bank or the investment company.

If the fees or commissions that you pay for performing financial transactions are not low enough, you may find out (especially in regard to the solid part of your investment portfolio) that it actually isn't financially worthwhile for you perform any activities (such as buying or selling securities) at all.

The aspect of cost is such an important part of your portfolio management that if you don't get the proper conditions, the only ones who will enjoy and profit from your financial transactions will be the financial institutions you work with.

The infrastructure upon which to base your private investment portfolio

Connect to your bank account or investment company account online

When you run a private investment portfolio it is important to have real-time access to information and to be able to sell and buy financial products independently.

It is recommended that you fill out all of the necessary documents that will allow you to operate online, in advance. This way, you won't have to depend on the availability of an advisor or wait for a confirmatory phone call to carry out transactions on the stock exchange. Another advantage of online transactions is the availability of excellent trading platforms that provide added value to the management of your investment portfolio.

Consulting agreement

If you are working with a financial institution that allows you to consult with a licensed investment advisor, you should consider signing an agreement to do so. Without a signed agreement, it is not possible to actually use the consulting services of the bank/investment company. When signing the consulting agreement, the financial advisor will ask you questions related to your profile as an investor, such as the level of risk you wish to take and the length of time that the money will be invested. Your answers will be entered to a simulator and the advisor will print a document describing your investor profile and a general recommendation for the composition of your investment portfolio. Save a copy of this report and use it as a tool to manage your investment portfolio.

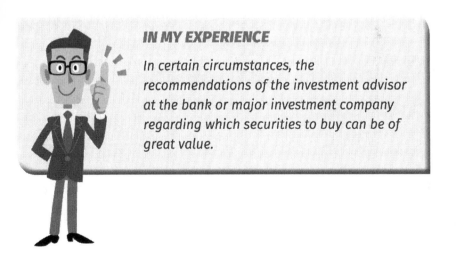

IN MY EXPERIENCE

In certain circumstances, the recommendations of the investment advisor at the bank or major investment company regarding which securities to buy can be of great value.

Why? Because these recommendations are often made from a relatively small list of recommended securities, built by the bank's or the investment company's research department. The consultants at these institutions make recommendations based on this same list to thousands of customers on a weekly basis. Because thousands of people are given these recommendations and act accordingly, it is possible to predict situations in which specific stocks (from the list) will rise significantly. In essence, the effect is that of a self-fulfilling prophesy.

If you decide to follow the recommendations given, it is important to buy only the recommended stocks that do not yet display a sharp rise. How? Ask what the target price of each security is and by how much their price has already increased; the securities you should consider are those that have only started to rise and are still well below their target price.

Make sure the fees related to your investment portfolio are low

The ultimatum technique to lower commissions

In every financial activity, you're involved in, it's important to make sure you know in advance exactly what fees you are going to pay.

Why are low commissions so important?

First, high commissions can impact the advisability of a transaction, sometimes to the point that the transaction should not be carried out at all.

Second, almost all of the commissions charged by the bank can be negotiated. If you know what you're expected to pay, you can ask to considerably reduce the commission. The "ultimatum technique": tell your bank or investment company that their competitors offered you a lower commission for your investment account and say that if they don't match those conditions then you'll transfer all your money to their competitors. But don't bluff - it is important to mention the specific name of the bank / investment company that offered you the low commission.

Fees for securities

As mentioned above, the level of commission for buying and selling securities and financial products is very important for your financial activity. A long series of transactions in securities brings with it a long series of transaction fees. The annual accumulation of these fees can add up to a considerable sum, reducing the profitability of your investment portfolio. Therefore, you should do anything you can to reduce those commissions as much as possible.

Foreign currency exchange fee

If you want to buy securities abroad, sometimes you have to use foreign currency. In this situation, you will have to first convert some of your money to the foreign currency, often from dollars to euros, paying a fee to do so. When buying a foreign currency, it is important to pay the lowest exchange fee possible; when you sell the foreign currency, it's important you get the highest rate on the exchange as possible.

Service quality

Although the commission you pay is important, the quality of service you get is also a significant factor. The quality of service is measured by availability, professionalism and the reliability of the information you receive, and especially, by the quality of the investment consultants available to you. It is therefore important that you choose the advisor that best suits your needs before beginning to operate your investment portfolio.

The preferred advisor should be one with many years of experience and one with whom you communicate well. Talk with the investment advisor and check what background and experience they have. See if you share a common language. Many institution branches have more than one investment advisor - choose the one you connect to and feel comfortable working with.

The advantages of having a financial advisor

Reports and recommendations

The advisor has access to the reports prepared by the economics department of the financial institution at which they are employed. These reports can provide essential information on the basis of which you can determine, among other things, how much foreign currency you should keep in your investment portfolio; as well as the institution recommendation regarding the percentage to invest in various investment channels.

Support for financial decisions

If you already decided to buy a particular security, you can consult with the advisor to make sure they support your decision.

Discounts when buying financial products

An advisor at a large bank or investment company has the power and ability to buy financial products at a discount. Such a discount can sometimes save you a significant amount of money.

Help with buying and selling

If you are a new investor and don't have a lot of experience in buying and selling securities, the advisor can provide you with technical support.

Consultations regarding market trends

You can ask the advisor their opinion about market trends and discuss the various issues that arise while you are managing your own portfolio.

BE AWARE!

The advisor's strength lies in their ability to help you choose an investment product that best suits your needs, especially if you taking your first steps in the investment world. The importance of the advisor's role is especially notable when you know what you want to do, but not know how to do it - i.e., what investment product to choose.

Suppose you've decided to invest some of your money in real estate securities: the advisor will be able to show you a variety of options in real estate stock available for investment, and explain the costs associated with each option as well as other criteria, such as return verses risk.

Example: A recommendation for the composition of an investment portfolio

Investor: *"What is the recommendation of your economics department regarding the optimal distribution of investment channels in an investment portfolio?"*

Consultant: *"To answer your question I need to ask you some questions and enter your replies in our financial simulator - I need to know the level of risk you are interested in: low, medium, or high; and for what period of time you intend to hold the investment?"*

Investor: *"I see my investment horizon as between 5 and 8 years, and I want to invest in high-risk investments."*

Consultant: *"I printed out a report that includes my recommendations* *regarding the percentage of investment in each channel and lists a number of financial products relevant to each channel."*

Practical Conclusions

It is important to make sure that the fees related to the management of your private investment portfolio are minimal. If you don't, then the commissions you pay for your financial activity while managing your investment portfolio will generate nice profits for your bank or investment company - and your profitability as an investor will be low.

Even if you are used to working alone, you can still use some of the services offered by an investment advisor. The advantages to consulting with an advisor lie not only in the advice they give you, but also in their access to central, sophisticated sources of important information.

The 4th practice of the 1%

Using core-satellite asset allocation strategy

What is asset allocation?

Asset allocation is the implementation of an investment strategy in an investment portfolio. The strategy attempts to balance risk versus reward by adjusting the percentage of each asset in your investment portfolio according to your personal preferences, the market conditions and the economic environment. The main assumption in asset allocation is that the investment in different assets results in portfolio diversification, which reduces the overall risk in your investment portfolio while maintaining the level of the expected return.

Core-satellite asset allocation

Core-satellite allocation strategy defines a "core" strategic element that comprises the most significant portion of the portfolio, and applies a dynamic "satellite" strategy to the smaller part of the portfolio.

The "core" portion of the portfolio incorporates passive investments that don't require dynamic handling (i.e. index funds, exchange-traded funds (ETFs), mutual passive funds) while the "satellite" portion of the portfolio is composed of investments that demand a more dynamic approach. In the satellite portion, you adjust your portfolio to include the assets, sectors, or individual stocks that show the most potential for gains. The expectation is that the satellite portion of your portfolio will outperform the market benchmark.

Before you implement the core-satellite asset allocation strategy, you have to define what your preferences are as an investor. The portfolio should be built in accordance with your desires and needs; to accomplish this, you need to address the following issues:

The sum of money you are going to invest in your private portfolio

You have to determine the appropriate amount of money to invest in the capital market. To do this, you must also consider your other assets and the level of risk to which they are exposed.

The investment horizon

The longer the investment horizon, the higher the level of risk you can afford to be exposed to, since your investments will have plenty of time to ride out the market's short-term fluctuations. Accordingly, the potential to gain higher returns will be greater.

If, for example, you know in advance that you are going to purchase an asset within the next two years – then you shouldn't use this money to invest in the capital market. Why? Because it is possible that the capital market will decline sharply during those two years: since you will be forced to sell your investment in order to buy the asset, you will not be able to wait for the market to rise, and you will lose money on your investment.

Exposure to risk and required return

As an investor, you should decide what weight (percentage) to give the risky and the solid parts of your portfolio. A simple investment strategy is to keep all of your money in US treasury bonds, which have a guaranteed return: the obvious advantage of this strategy is that it's a safe investment with almost no risk, while the disadvantage is that the return on such an investment will accordingly be very low. If, however, you are an investor who is willing to take some risk, investment in stocks and corporate bonds will increase your chances of earning more money. The relationship between return/reward and risk is a double-edged sword: to profit more, you have to be willing to take more risk.

For example, even if you are a very aggressive investor who is willing to take big risks, you may find that in certain financial market environments you'll prefer to keep a low percentage of stocks in your portfolio (and put most of your money in US treasury bonds), based on your impression that there is currently no positive horizon for the stock market.

Exposure to foreign markets and currencies

You also need to decide whether you want to expose your investment portfolio to domestic and / or foreign, developed or emerging markets. Note that if you buy ETFs traded in a foreign country, they in most cases will be influenced by the currency exchange of that country; therefore, your investment returns will also be influenced by the exchange rate. Meaning, buying ETFs on overseas stock indexes exposes you to foreign currency fluctuations.

Financial products that can be included in the solid part of the portfolio

Government bonds:

- Short- and medium-term, up to 5 years.

- Corporate bonds: with high ratings (AA or higher); short- or medium-term, up to five years.

- Mutual bonds funds: with high ratings and an average maturity of up to 5 years.

Cash and cash equivalents:

- Deposit accounts

- Short-term government bonds

- Money market funds

- Certificates of deposit (CDs - including foreign currency)

Financial products that can be included in the risky part of the portfolio

- Stocks

- Long-term bonds with an average maturity of over 5 years; bonds rated A or lower

- Corporate junk bonds with high yield

- REITs (commercial or residential real estate)

- Convertible bonds

- Warrants

- Options

- Mutual funds

- Stock-oriented funds

- ETFs on branches

- Commodities (such as gold and silver); and more.

BE AWARE!

You can easily find free, good-quality simulators that can be used to simulate asset allocations based on your preferences while taking the macroeconomic conditions in the market into account.

For example, in an economy with low interest rates the simulator recommendation may be to invest in short- and medium-term bonds only. Another example - it is possible that, based on global economic considerations, the recommendation will be to focus more on investments in the United States and Europe and less on China and developing countries; of course, the opposite is also possible. In addition to the simulators, you can seek the assistance of a licensed financial advisor.

Practical Conclusions

Core-satellite investing strategy is a powerful method for asset allocation. The decision to use this strategy to build your private investment portfolio can be the principal determinant of your investment results, and is therefore one of the most important decisions that you, as an investor, can make.

The 5th practice of the 1%

Build your risky investments as an independent entity

There are two advantages to building the risky part of your investment portfolio separately from the solid part:

First, the technical management of the portfolio is simplified and therefore easier to understand. Second, it's easier to measure the performance of the portfolio against market benchmarks: the risky part is compared to the performance of the stock market and high-yield bonds, and the solid part is compared to the benchmark of solid bonds.

Portfolio Construction: Building the risky part of the portfolio

Stage 1

Deciding the characteristics of the portfolio

Parameters: the sum of money to invest, the level of risk, the investment horizon, and the investment strategy.

For example:

- **The sum of all portfolio investment:** $200,000
- **Moderate risk:** up to 50% (the risky part)
- **The investment horizon:** 20 years
- **The investment strategy:** Core-satellite investing

BE AWARE!

The "market portfolio" is a theoretical concept. It is defined as a portfolio consisting of investments that includes every financial asset available in the world market. The representation of each asset in the "market portfolio" is proportional to its total presence in the world market.

Because its components mirror all of the assets in the financial world, the expected return of the market portfolio should be identical to the expected return of the whole market. Since the market portfolio, by definition, is optimally diversified, it is subject only to risks that affect the whole market, and not to the risks relevant to a particular asset in the portfolio. In the process of building an investment portfolio based on the "market portfolio" concept, investors use proxies for the market portfolio such as the S&P 500 in the US, the FTSE 100 in the UK, the DAX in Germany and more.

Stage 2

Building the core portion of your portfolio

The "core" will be built from passively managed investments that approximately represent the "market portfolio."

The goal - The expected returns will be similar to the returns of the "market portfolio".

For example:

- $40,000 in a ETF on the S&P 500 (40%)
- $10,000 in a European mutual index fund (10%)
- $10,000 in an ETF on the NASDAQ (10%)

Stage 3

Construction of the dynamic element – the satellite

The satellite portion will be built from actively managed investments. These are investments that do not reflect the "market portfolio".

The goal: The expected returns should outperform the returns of the "market portfolio."

For example:

- $15,000 in a REIT (real estate investment trust) ETF (15%)
- $10,000 in a Gold ETF (10%)
- $5,000 in a mutual fund specializing in high-dividend stocks (5%)
- $5,000 in junk bonds with high yields (5%)
- $5,000 in a mutual fund specializing in green energy (5%)

Warning!!!

The securities mentioned here are only examples and do not represent suggestions or any recommendation for what you should or should not invest in. It is highly recommended that you build your private investment portfolio with the help of a licensed financial advisor.

4 Insights regarding building a portfolio using the core-satellite method

Insight #1
The composition of the core creates two key advantages:

Minimized costs and minimized risk

The first advantage is that the "core" is made up of passively managed securities, and the managing fees charged by portfolio managers, as well as the transaction costs, are considerably less expensive than for active investments.

The second advantage is that the "core" is composed of investments (index funds, ETFs, passive mutual funds) that approximately represent the "market portfolio"; therefore, there is a close to optimal diversification of the portfolio. The diversification ensures reduced volatility, meaning the overall risk of the investment portfolio is reduced.

Insight #2
The satellite investments should outperform the benchmark of the "market portfolio".

Maximize returns

The satellite portion consists of active investments that are considerably more expensive than the passive investments. The only justification for the higher price to be paid when investing in actively managed investments is the assumption that the portfolio manager will manage the investments so that the overall returns of the entire portfolio beat the market benchmark. If not, then all of the money would be better invested in passive investments.

Insight #3
Some of the satellite investments should reduce the risk of the entire portfolio.

Minimize volatility

When managing the satellite investment portion, you must consider the portfolio as a whole. The financial markets have periods of uncertainty that increase the volatility of the market. Gold is one of the financial means to reduce this volatility, since in most cases, the prices of gold will rise when there is uncertainty in the market. Adding an investment such as a gold ETF, which can move in a direction opposite that of the stock market, helps limit the overall volatility of the investment portfolio as a whole when the markets are not stable.

In addition to gold there are other, alternative assets that can contribute added value to the whole portfolio, such as hedge funds, REITs, options, and foreign currencies.

Insight #4
How can you select the best ETFs or mutual funds?

The criteria – benchmark, Sharpe ratio, & costs.

Although the core is composed of passively managed investments and has a reduced cost compered to active investments, it will serve the profitability of your portfolio to reduce its associated costs even further. Therefore, the basis for selecting a passive mutual fund or ETF should be their cost.

In the satellite portion, however, the selection of financial products is more sophisticated: selections in the active part of your portfolio should be based on one of three things, or a combination of them:

1. The benchmark.
2. The Sharpe ratio.
3. The cost.

IN MY EXPERIENCE

The satellite portion of the portfolio can also reflect your personal values.

For example, if preserving the Earth is important to you, you can express that value by investing some of your money in a mutual fund that deals with renewable energy that is less harmful to the planet. If you love the military, you can invest in a mutual fund related to the army. If you are an advanced technology and robots freak, you can act accordingly. The idea is that you can choose to invest in sectors based on your personal values and interests.

Practical Conclusions

Core-satellite investment strategy is a method of portfolio construction that enables you to minimize costs and volatility and provides you with an opportunity to build your private investment portfolio to outperform the market benchmark.

A core-satellite investment strategy can reflect your personal style or values: for example, you can invest most of your money in the domestic market as opposed to foreign markets, or favor some investment sectors over others.

The 6th practice of the 1%

Build your solid investments as an independent entity

Portfolio Construction: Building the solid part of the portfolio

Stage 1

Deciding the characteristics of the portfolio

Parameters: the sum of money to invest, the level of risk, the investment horizon, and the investment strategy.

for example:

- **The sum of all portfolio investment:** $200,000
- **The size of the solid part:** up to 50%
- **The investment horizon:** 20 years
- **The investment strategy:** Core-satellite investing

Stage 2

Building the core portion of your portfolio

The "core" will be built from passively managed investments that approximately represent the "market portfolio" of solid investments.

The goal - The expected returns will be similar to the returns of the "solid market portfolio".

for example:

- $40,000 (40%) in an ETF in US government bonds
- $20,000 (20%) in a money market fund

Stage 3

Construction of the dynamic element – the satellite

The satellite portion will be built from actively managed bond investments.

The goal - The expected returns should outperform the returns of the core portion.

for example:

- $30,000 (30%) in an ETF in corporate US bonds
- $5,000 (5%) in a mutual fund specializing in corporate bonds in England
- $5,000 (5%) in a mutual fund specializing in corporate bonds in Germany

NOTE: All of the bonds in the solid part should meet two criteria: first, the bonds should have an average maturity of up to 5 years or less. Second, the corporate bonds should have high ratings (AA or higher). Bonds that do not meet those criteria are not considered solid investments.

Warning!!!

The securities mentioned here are only examples and do not represent suggestions or any recommendation for what you should or should not invest in. It is highly recommended that you build your private investment portfolio with the help of a licensed financial advisor.

Insights regarding building a portfolio using the core-satellite method

Insight #1
The importance of liquidity

Liquidity refers to the portion of the portfolio that you can immediately realize to cash without a loss in return. Although you receive very low returns from the liquid portion, it's an important part of the overall investment portfolio. The liquidity allows you to act quickly if there are opportunities in the financial market. If you need a high level of liquidity, then cash and cash equivalents can meet this requirement.

Insight #2
Exposure to foreign markets and currencies

If you buy ETFs traded in a foreign country, they in most cases will be influenced by the currency exchange of that country. Therefore, buying ETFs on overseas stock indexes exposes you to foreign currency fluctuations.

Insight #3
Use the Sharpe ratio to buy excellent mutual bond funds

When you want to buy cooperate bonds, it's a good idea to do so using a professional mutual fund that excels at managing bond investment portfolios. The fee that you will pay them will be minimal compared to the time and resources that you would have to invest to deal with cooperate bond buying and management on your own.

BE AWARE!

There is a fundamental difference between bonds and shares, which in most cases makes bonds a less risky alternative. Unlike bonds, company shares have no "guaranteed return." In other words, they do not guarantee a predictable cash flow to be paid on a specified future date.

When you hold shares, you rely on their market value. When you hold bonds, you have a chance to get the "guaranteed return" even if the company suffers financial difficulties or bankruptcy; the company shareholders, in contrast, can lose all their money.

As you can see, the solid portion of the portfolio consists mostly of bonds. It is recommended to use mutual funds that specialize in managing bonds as part of your investment portfolio. But just so you know what's what, following is a concise explanation regarding bonds:

A bond - a loan you give the government or a company

When you invest in bonds, you are essentially giving a loan to the government (government bonds) or a publicly traded company (corporate bonds). In return, you receive a guaranteed, predictable cash income which will be paid on a specified future date. The "guaranteed return" is paid by the body that issued the bond (the government or company).

For example: If you purchased a cooperate bond that has 5 years to maturity and an annual coupon of 7%, then you have a guarantee that you will receive a coupon of 7% each year. You can consider it a loan that you gave to the company that gives you a 7% interest rate on your money every year. The original bond sum is returned to you upon completion of the 5-year period.

Government bonds are always safer than corporate bonds:

The government can always print more money to meet its obligations, while companies depend on their financial strength to meet their obligations.

Bond ratings:

Cooperate bonds are rated according to their level of risk. The rating is given by professional companies who specialize in the topic. The rating provides investors with information regarding the risk of investing in various bonds.

If the rating of a bond is low, its means is that the probability that you could lose all your money is high. The expected interest on such a low-rated bond is very high - some investors are willing to take the chance and buy low-rated (dangerous) bonds: the compensation for the additional risk that those investors take is called the "risk premium". This is why corporate junk bonds are also called high-yield bonds.

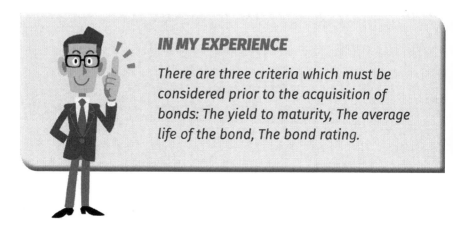

IN MY EXPERIENCE

There are three criteria which must be considered prior to the acquisition of bonds: The yield to maturity, The average life of the bond, The bond rating.

1. **The yield to maturity:** The annual return of the investor, if the bond is held until maturity.
2. **The average life of the bond:** The average duration, in annual terms, of the bond. The longer the term, the riskier the bond.
3. **The bond rating:** A rating which indicates the probability that the borrower (the government / cooperation) will meet its obligations and return the invested money + the promised interest.

Practical Conclusions

There are two major challenges which you face as an investor.

The first challenge presents when the financial markets are in flux (inflation, currency fluctuations, interest rate changes, etc.): in such circumstances, you must know how to respond effectively to the changing market conditions. An investor who does not respond appropriately may suffer significant losses.

The second challenge you face as an investor is dealing and communicating with the representatives of the financial institutions that hold your money, such as banks and investment companies. Their representatives can give you valuable input if you know how to interact with them and ask the right questions; but bear in mind that they get their salaries and bonuses from the institutions they work for, and won't necessarily give you the advice that works best for you.

Your ability to manage your private investment portfolio gives you powerful tools that enable you to meet these two important challenges.

The 7th practice of the 1%

Choosing and using the best funds and ETFs

Choosing and using the best funds and exchange traded funds (ETFs) as an integral part of your investment portfolio

Basically, your personal investment portfolio can be constructed by selecting individual securities. This will require a great deal of time and energy: it can take many years to acquire sufficient financial knowledge in just one sector or field. For example, it takes years to specialize in managing bond portfolios or to become an expert in a specific sector - the biotechnology or technology sector, for instance. Even if you have the appropriate knowledge, you will need to conduct routine maintenance on every security you buy, which includes the ongoing monitoring of the company's structure and business progress; stay updated regrading relevant Press and Stock Exchange Releases; and in addition, follow the changes in the sector of the security you are holding. It's safe to assume that the considerable time and energy that you'll invest in such intensive activity will impact your abilities to manage your investment portfolio as a whole.

The practical, effective solution is the integration of ETFs and mutual funds to your portfolio. You should select the best mutual funds with the best investment managers in every field, and your focus should be on the overall management of your investment portfolio.

IN MY EXPERIENCE

You can take a relatively small amount of money and use it to buy individual securities. As an example, let's assume you have a portfolio of $500,000. You decide that $20,000 will be invested in 4 securities at $5,000 each.

The decision in what shares to invest this money can be based on your personal preferences and on the potential of each specific share in the relevant categories to rise in the future.

What is a mutual fund?

In essence, mutual funds are joint investments. They pool money from many investors to purchase securities, which include stocks, bonds, money market instruments and similar assets. When you invest your money in a mutual fund, it allows you to use licensed portfolio managers to manage your investment and thereby benefit from their knowledge and experience. Even if you invest $2,000 and another investor invests $50,000, you will receive the same treatment.

What is an ETF?

An ETF (exchange traded fund) is a marketable security that tracks an index, a commodity, bonds or a basket of assets. Like a mutual fund, an ETF is a pool of investments; however, an ETF will often have lower associated costs. Unlike mutual funds, an ETF trades like a common stock on the stock exchange, and its price changes throughout the day as it is bought and sold.

Investment diversification of mutual funds and ETFs

Investing in mutual funds and ETFs takes advantage of the golden rule - "don't put all your eggs in one basket". Thanks to their diversification, you can get maximum returns with minimum risk.

BE AWARE!

Although ETFs have no active management fees, they do have operational fees. Therefore, it's important to choose the ETFs with the lowest costs. Another important consideration when buying ETFs is their marketability - the ease with which you can buy and sell them at market price when you choose.

The main advantage of investing through a mutual fund:

Mutual funds have portfolio managers, who have extensive knowledge of the capital market and securities. If you buy a mutual fund in a specific sector it is reasonable to assume that the managers of the fund are experts in the sector that the mutual fund belongs to (for example – biotechnology, or fashion, or cooperate bonds). The portfolio manager takes into account all of the conditions and factors that affect the stock exchange of the specific industry that the mutual fund belongs to. He monitors industry and economic trends, searches for the right company in which to invest the portfolio's capital, and determines the appropriate time to do so. His motivation is to beat the market benchmark and compete successfully with others who manage similar mutual funds.

Why are ETFs sometimes a better choice?

Mutual funds have been a popular way to invest for several decades, whereas ETFs are relatively new. The popularity of

ETFs is based on three factors: lower cost, better tax treatment and at times, better returns compared to mutual funds.

The question arises as to whether the fees for active management charged by the mutual fund are justified. The answer is that the fees are justified only if the annual returns you get on the fund, after payment of the fees, are higher than the returns you would have gained if you had bought an ETF, minus its cost. In many cases, ETFs that mimic indexes, like the S&P 500 index, give higher returns than mutual funds.

IN MY EXPERIENCE

Although in most cases, actively managed portfolios will not produce higher returns than an ETF, it is often better to use an active mutual fund when investing in niche industries or sectors.

Portfolio management when investing in mutual funds and ETFs

The power of your flexibility

You can think of mutual funds or ETFs like a train running along the market's trend line (i.e. the "tracks"). You, the investor in these funds / ETFs, are not the driver, but a passenger who can choose when to get on the train (buy), when to stay on the train (hold) and when to get off (sell); in addition to buying and selling, you can also decide how much money to invest. The published returns of the funds / ETFs are not necessarily equal to your return: your return will depend only on your financial decisions that determine the timing and the amount of your investment.

The timing of your investments

As an investor who manages his own personal investment portfolio, you should decide during which periods of time to invest in mutual funds / ETFs. If you think the market is doing well, increase your exposure to risky assets by purchasing riskier funds / ETFs in the satellite portion of your portfolio. When you see that the market is saturated and coming close to peaking, minimize your exposure to risk by moving your money to solid mutual funds or solid ETFs. When the stock market is doing poorly, maintain liquidity in the solid (low-risk) channel.

If you think the market is at the end of its recession period and you have the opportunity to buy securities at low prices, then increase your exposure to risky securities. How? Transfer some of your money from the solid funds /ETFs to more aggressive funds / ETFs. Don't try for high accuracy in timing, i.e. to purchase securities at a low price and sell them at a high price: these attempts will likely result in financial damage. Instead, focus on managing your exposure to stocks/risk according to your personal preferences and the changing market conditions. If necessary, "wait it out" until better times.

How to buy the best mutual funds and ETFs

When you want to buy a mutual fund or an ETF, buy only the best ones. How can you determine which ones are the best? Use the following powerful tools and criteria:

- **The Sharpe ratio** – The ratio of the fund / ETF you're considering should be high compared to that of others
- **The benchmark** – The benchmark of the fund / ETF you're considering should be the same as or higher than that of others
- **Low cost** – The cost should be low as possible

Simulation: choosing a mutual fund

Client: *"I want t*o invest $15,000 in the information security sector. Can you give me a list of the best ones based on the Sharpe ratio?"

Advisor: "No problem, I have a list of the 10 leading funds in the information security sector; the best ones are at the top of the list."

Client: "Please purchas*e the top 3 in the list for me. I'd like to invest $5,000 in each one."*

Practical Conclusions

When you build your investment portfolio it is recommended to use ETFs and mutual funds as financial instruments.

This will give you the ability to concentrate on making decisions regarding asset allocation in a changing market while looking at your investment portfolio as a whole. When you buy ETFs or mutual funds, choose them wisely. Use at least one of the three parameters of cost, benchmark, and Sharpe ratio. The end result will be that out of the thousands of mutual funds offered in the financial market, your investment portfolio will contain the ones with the best performance.

The 8th practice of the 1%

Profit from the expertise of financial institutions

The limitations of the financial institutions

We can profit from the expertise of financial institutions by holding excellent products that they manage (for example, mutual funds) in our investment portfolio. At the same time, however, we have to acknowledge that they have disadvantages. Below is a list of considerations, limitations and constraints that present in the financial institutions, which we have to identify and neutralize.

Limitations related to market trends

The investment manager of a financial institution must act in accordance with current trends. Take, for example, a situation in which the stock and the bond markets have already reached their peaks and are priced very high. Let's suppose the investment manager thinks that there is a high probability that the market will drop, and that now is therefore the optimal time to reduce exposure to stocks and corporate bonds. The public, however, is not yet aware of the financial danger and continues to make massive acquisitions of financial products that contain stocks and bonds. As a result of the high demand, the market continues to rise. Therefore, the investment manager will have to purchase securities at a high market price, even though he believes that buying them at that time is not profitable. In other words, in such circumstances the investment manager is forced to act contrary to his professional judgment.

Now let's assume that the market is declining, and the public - out of fear - is selling expensive financial products. As a result, prices in the bond and stock market decline sharply. Suppose the investment manager thinks that with such low prices, now is the time to purchase these securities: even so, if the general public continues to sell financial products, he too will be forced to sell securities at low prices, in order to have money available for the clients who sold their securities. In this example as well, the investment manager is forced to act contrary to his professional judgment

IN MY EXPERIENCE

It could be argued, and rightly so, that the majority of the public is ignorant regarding financial risk. The public invests a large amount of money , with the expectation of high returns, when the market is at its height - while choosing to ignore potential risks.

The general public has a tendency to enter the market when it is already at its peak, after a period of significant rise; decisions are made impulsively, based mainly on personal feelings and on information obtained from various media channels. In this reality, financial institutions know that they must generate returns even if doing so involves taking high risks - otherwise, the investors will leave them for their competitors.

Limitations related to response time

In difficult times, the ability of large financial institutions that manage large sums of money to respond in real time is very limited due to their size. If, for example, there is concern that a specific sector is about to drop, they will start the process of realizing/selling the holdings of this dangerous sector, but because they fear that their massive sellings will themselves affect the market and bring down the stocks, they will work slowly and in stages.

For example: if a big investment institution invested a large sum of money in banking sector shares and for some reason wants to eliminate those shares, it will do so in stages. If they sell all their holdings at once, the stocks prices might fall as a result of the significant sell-off – because the financial institution is a major player in the market.

When buying securities, the reaction time of the large financial institutions is also slow; in this case, the management of the portfolio is less effective, since effective investment management requires a real-time response to what is happening in the market.

Furthermore, large financial institutions cannot invest in shares that belong to companies considered relatively small: the very act of buying such a share will result in a significant increase in the share market price.

This is the reason why large investment companies cannot be too creative or buy "interesting securities" - for example, they cannot add shares of a technology company whose market value is only $30 million dollars to their portfolio. They are limited to buying the shares of medium and large companies.

Limitations related to a built-in policy

Financial products have built-in polices that restrict them: the ability of portfolio managers who manage mutual funds to respond to market conditions, by reducing exposure to risk, for instance, is limited. For example, the manager of a mutual fund must act according to the policy that appears in the prospectus of that mutual fund. For instance, if the prospectus says that the mutual fund has to hold a minimum of 70% shares, no matter what the market conditions, then the investment manager must comply.

Considerations regarding competition with other financial institutions

In certain periods, a portfolio manager may decide that it is prudent to reduce exposure to risky securities, and do so, in order to protect his client's money. But unfortunately for him the stock market has a life of its own: the stock market may rise during the same period, meaning that in retrospect, the investment manager prediction was wrong. The impact of such a wrong prediction can result in some of his customers leaving. Why? Because his customers judge his performance by comparing the returns that he generates with the returns of other firms. If they see that his performance is weak compared to other investments companies, they may decide to switch to a competitor who earned more - not knowing that it's because he didn't reduce his clients exposure to risk.

The opposite scenario is also possible - if the portfolio manager does not reduce the risk (even though he thinks it's the right time to do so) and then in retrospect it turns out he was right - and the market indeed dropped, causing his customers to incur losses - he know their customers will "forgive him". Why? Because his competitors also suffered similar losses.

Conclusion:

Since portfolio managers are aware of how the public thinks and acts, they do not necessarily act to reduce risk, even if they think that it is appropriate to do so.

BE AWARE!

The investment managers in financial institutions are sometimes more afraid of the competition from other investment companies than the risks of the financial market. Their first and foremost fear is to look worse than their competitors.

A portfolio manager knows that his performance is always compared to that of other managers. Therefore, even if his professional opinion is that the financial market is in danger he will not necessarily reduce exposure to risk, but rather chooses to act like his competitors.

Disabling the constraints and profiting from the opportunities

As noted, the investment managers at financial institutions have limitations that may lead them to operate contrary to their professional judgement. But these restrictions are not applicable to you: you can always sell the fund / ETF. You, and only you, have the responsibility to get rid of the fund / ETF or reduce your exposure to risk, thus reducing the damage that may be caused to your money. For example, in good times you should increase your exposure to funds / ETF shares, and in challenging times you should reduce exposure and move to more conservative funds. When the market reaches low price levels, indicating, among others things, the panic in the general public, you can take advantage of the situation and buy funds / ETFs to collect stocks at attractive prices.

Practical Conclusions

The portfolio managers of various financial institutions have professional knowledge and expertise that that you can profit from. But at the same time, they also have several significant limitations. When managing your own private investment portfolio, you need to know how to benefit from their advantages (such as the purchase of excellent leading mutual funds for your private portfolio); while remaining aware of their limitations. You - and you alone - are responsible for counteracting those limitations; and if you do so – then you will earn significantly more on your money.

The 9th practice of the 1%

Avoiding exotic financial products

There are thousands of companies and individuals around the world who offer financial solutions for making easy money. In most cases, they are registered in, and operate from, countries/zones with no financial regulation. Basically, their only goal is to take your money. They know how to accurately identify your financial goals and needs and they will do anything to move your money from your bank account to their pocket. Their only real expertise is in the psychology of people. When they communicate with you, they convey total confidence; they are masters of the art of temptation. Their unregulated financial products contain a lot of false promises.

BE AWARE!

Every financial product that someone tries to sell you must meet three basic conditions:
1. *It must be sold by a licensed financial entity (a bank, an investment company), preferably a financial institution that exists in the country you live in;*
2. *The money to purchase the product must remain in a bank account registered in your name, i.e. there is no demand that you transfer your money to another account; and*
3. *The product is simple and easy to understand.*

A good analogy can be - hot dogs. Although hot dogs look good and make you want to eat them, you can assume that they're made using cheap, unhealthy ingredients. There are financial products that are difficult to understand, introduced as "sexy" and profitable, which are indeed composed of elements that are very profitable - but only to the seller. If you give into temptation and buy them, they can hurt the returns in your investment portfolio.

What is Forex?

The Foreign Exchange global market, where currencies are traded.

It is decentralized, meaning there is no central marketplace for foreign exchange; instead, currency trading is conducted electronically over the counter (OTC), - all transactions between traders occur via computer networks around the world. The market is open 24 hours a day except on weekends. The foreign exchange market assists international trade and business by providing a platform for currency conversion. For example, if you live in the US and you want to buy a car from Germany you have to pay for the car in euros (EUR).

Forex encompasses several markets: the spot market, the forwards market and the futures market. When people talk about the forex market, they are most often referring to the spot market: the spot market is where currencies are bought and sold according to the current price. The current price is a reflection of many variables. The forwards and the futures markets are used by international corporations to protect them against future fluctuations in exchange rates.

Why are private forex companies dangerous for your money?

There are many private forex companies that want you to use their platform for trading. They promise you a quick way to make a lot of money in a short period of time, with a relatively small investment. They teach their clients how to speculate on currency values and emphasize the ability of the company to use leverage to enhance profits. What happens in reality is that over time their customers lose all of their money! This happens because of one very important fact - the forex market is decentralized, and is under little supervision (if any) by regulatory bodies.

What are binary options?

A binary option is a financial option in which the payoff is either a defined, fixed monetary amount - or nothing at all. Binary options are used in a theoretical framework as the building block for asset pricing and financial derivatives.

What are the implications of a non-regulated binary option market on trading?

Many unregulated binary markets are being traded on the internet; these are likely to be scams. The binary option "brokers" do not operate from a real brokerage; the customer is betting against the broker. The brokers manipulate price data to mislead their customers, and withdrawals are regularly stalled or refused. On non-regulated platforms, the client's money, in most cases, is not kept in a trust account, as required by government financial regulation, and transactions are not monitored by third parties in order to ensure fair play.

Structured products

Most structured products appear to have a magical quality - you can be exposed to risky securities that generate more profit, and at the same time, stay protected. There are countries in Europe where structured products are sold in post offices and sometimes even in supermarkets. At first glance, this product looks very tempting: apparently, you can expose yourself to the stock market and enjoy a profit if the shares rise, but even if the opposite happens and the shares decline, your protection is guaranteed - you'll still receive the principle. Even in the worst-case scenario, your money is safe. But as you will see, this is a sham. As the saying goes – nothing in life is free.

What is a structured product?

Also known as a market-linked investment, a structured product is created through a process of financial engineering. It is a pre-packaged investment strategy based on a combination of underlying factors such as shares, bonds, indices or commodities with derivatives (like options, forwards, and swaps).

IN MY EXPERIENCE

When they decided to build structured products, one of the main goals of investment banks was to increase their profit margins: since those products with added features were harder to value, it was thus harder to gauge the profits of the bank.

For example, if a bank sell a structured product to the public at a total sum of $100 million, they can take a hidden commission of 1% - equal to $1 million. The rest of the money - $99 million - could be invested in financial products that would enable them to meet their obligations to the customers. In most cases, when the customer buys the product he isn't aware of their hidden cost.

The general characteristics of a structure:

A guaranteed principal (in most cases)

You enjoy the potential to gain high / enhanced returns on an investment, while at the same time, the principal is protected. A feature of many structured products is a "principal guarantee" function, which offers protection of principal if held to maturity.

For example, the deposit can be linked to the S&P 500, and the conditions of the structure will be as follows: you will receive 70% of the increase (if obtained) at the end of two years. Even if the S&P 500 goes down, your investment (the principle) is protected. For example - if the S&P 500 index has risen by 40% at the completion of 2 years, then you will receive a return of 28%. If the index is negative - for example, it has decreased by 30%, then your return will be zero: you will not suffer any loss. In both cases, you have a guaranteed principal.

Lack of liquidity

The money is put into a closed deposit, usually for a period of several years, and can't be liquidated. If during that period you see the index that the structure is linked to rises considerably, and you want to realize your profits by selling the structure, the terms of the product do not allow you to do so. You are obligated to wait until the end of the period, and by then all the increases that you could have enjoyed if you could have sold earlier might be lost following a change in the market trend.

Alternative interest loss

The alternative interest loss could be very significant. If, for example, the structure can be liquidated only after 5 years, and if we assume that we could get 2% interest from a solid investment each year, then we'll essentially lose 10% because of the structure. This loss is called the alternative interest loss. Of course, if the structure does well then this alternative loss won't be an issue. But many times, when investing in structures you only get the principle – the sum of money you invested in the beginning - making the topic of alternative loss highly relevant.

BE AWARE!

Purchasing a structured product is similar to purchasing a car - the average buyer is not interested in what materials the engine is made of; he is only interested in the advantages of that vehicle - the vehicle's ability to travel fast, comfortably and safely.

When considering the purchase of a structured product, your focus of interest should not be on the details of how the investment bank builds it behind the scenes (using "financial engineers"). As an investor, you should concentrate on the characteristics of the product.

To make an investment decision regarding investment in a structure, you have to ask the right questions:
- Which company built the product;
- Is the product regulated;

- What are the conditions of the structure - is the principle (the original sum you invested) protected;
- To what underlying securities is the structure exposed to;
- For how many years is the product (and therefore the money you invested) locked in, with no liquidity;
- How much profit will you receive if there is an increase in the underlying asset.

If you see that the structure is complicated and it is difficult to determine what the future returns will be, then don't buy it.

Practical Conclusions

Dealing with forex trading or binary options trading involves a double risk – the first stems from the very nature of the investments, which themselves are dangerous. The second is the fact that in most cases, these financial products are under no regulation - so the companies that try to sell us these financial products can manipulate you any way they choose. Overall, it isn't wise to invest your money in them.

In contrast, structured products can be used as an alternative to a direct investment, as part of the asset allocation strategy to reduce the risk exposure of your portfolio. But you have to be very cautious when you buy them: even if you decide to invest in them, do so only when the entity behind the product is a regulated company, such as a bank or a large investment company; and only invest a relatively small amount of money - in the range of several thousand dollars per structure. If it is difficult for you to understand the payoff features of the structured product and its risk characteristics - then don't buy it in the first place.

The 10th practice of the 1%

Understanding and using leading market indicators

An active government has several important economic obligations / objectives that it should actively pursue: high employment, price stability, and economic growth. One of the most significant factors that influences the achievement of these objectives is the use of monetary policy, of which the central bank is in charge of implementing. The main tool the central bank uses to achieve the economic objectives of the government is controlling interest rate levels.

What is a central bank?

A central bank is an institution that manages a state's currency, money supply, and interest rates; and uses monetary policy to achieve the objectives of the government. The responsibilities of the central bank include controlling and managing interest rates, setting the reserve requirement, and during times of financial crisis, helping the banking sector to function properly. In most countries, central banks also monitor and supervise financial institutions (including banks) to reduce the risk of reckless or fraudulent activities.

What is a "monetary policy"?

In the United States, the Federal Reserve is in charge of the monetary policy. The Federal Reserve has 4 main economic goals: to achieve maximum employment (close to 5% unemployment); to maintain stable prices (2-3% inflation per year); to keep interest rates relatively low; and to provide banks with liquidity that enables them to operate in a "healthy" way. To achieve all 4 goals the Federal Reserve uses a monetary policy, which is implemented through the actions of the central bank. The main "weapon" of the Federal Reserve is controlling, and if needed, changing the interest rate. It does this via financial activities such as buying or selling government bonds and changing the amount of money that banks are required to keep in their reserves. These activities have far-reaching implications for the economy, as they impact the interest rates on savings accounts, corporate bonds, student loans and mortgages.

Therefore, if after a month the interest rate rises (as expected), the market will be indifferent: the effect has already been expressed in the market prices. However, if there is a "surprise" that the market didn't expect - for example, there is no increase in interest rates, or the increase is greater than expected - then the market will react / adjust to the new reality accordingly.

Interest rates and your investment portfolio

When deciding where to invest your money, you have several alternatives. If you know that the solid channel offers you a high interest rate with only a very low risk, then you presumably will put most of your money in solid investments, such as government bonds. In such circumstances your motivation to put money into risky investments, such as stocks, will be low, and your level of exposure to risky assets will drop. The opposite is also true: the lower the interest rates are, the more willing you will be prepared to take more risks in order to generate higher returns, and the higher your level of exposure to risky assets will be. In conditions of low interest rates the demand for risky assets is higher, and the prices, accordingly, are also higher.

There are a number of leading financial indicators that influence your investment portfolio. Understanding and monitoring them will allow you to optimally manage your investment portfolio.

What are the leading financial indicators for managing your investment portfolio?

1. Consumer Price Index

The consumer price index (CPI) measures changes in the price of a market basket of consumer goods and services purchased by households. Changes in the CPI are used as measures of inflation.

How can it impact your investment portfolio?

If the increases in the CPI are small and the expectation of inflation is low, then the equity market and the bond market interpret it in a positive way: low inflation pressures lead to low interest rates. When there are large increases in the CPI, the bond market and the equity market will react negatively: high inflation is expected, which will lead to increased interest rates.

2. The GDP

The gross domestic product (GDP) is a measure of the total market value of all final goods and services produced in a period (quarterly or yearly).

How can it impact your investment portfolio?

When GDP growth is healthy and stems from strong business activity it will lead to higher corporate profits. As a result of the higher profits, the stock market will rise. If the GDP expands more than the economic forecasts, then it can lead to inflation pressures that will bring the bond market down. When the GDP expands less rapidly than the economic predictions, the bond market will rise.

3. Housing starts

Housing starts reflect the number of new, privately-owned houses on which construction has been started in a given period.

How can it impact your investment portfolio?

Changes in the rate of housing starts have a 3-dimensional effect: there are more jobs for construction workers – so they have more money to spend; after the home is sold, it generates revenues for the company that built it; and the buyer spends money on furnishing the house - e.g. furniture and appliances.

When housing starts decrease, the bond market rises, because the decrease signals low inflation pressures.

When housing starts increase, the bond market goes down because of the fear of inflation, while stock prices may react in a positive way because cooperate profits will rise.

4. Joblessness claims

This report tracks how many new people have filed for unemployment benefits in the previous week.

How can it impact your investment portfolio?

An increasing trend indicates that less people have jobs, so their ability to spend money is weakened. On the other hand, a decreasing trend indicates that more people have jobs: every job generates an income that gives the household more spending power, creating a stronger economy with more corporation profits. This is good for the stock market. But if the number of job seekers is so low that businesses have a hard time finding new workers, then they are forced to spend more on labor costs. This leads to wage inflation, which can be followed by an increase in interest rates, bringing down the stock and bond markets together.

5. Durable goods orders

An economic indicator that reflects the number of new orders placed with domestic manufacturers for the delivery of factory hard goods (in the near term or the future).

How can it impact your investment portfolio?

If the trend in durable goods orders is weak, the bonds market will rise because this signals low pressure on inflation. When the trend in durable goods orders is strong, there are two possible scenarios: in the first scenario, the indicator of durable goods orders shows a steady increase while at the same time, companies invest in equipment that enhances their capacity to increase production. Because they can meet the growing demand, the prospects for inflation are reduced.

Therefore, in this scenario, growing corporate profits will lead to rising share prices. In the second scenario, the durable goods indicator is high, but the demand for goods is higher than the supply: this can lead to inflation pressures that negatively influence the bond market.

IN MY EXPERIENCE

Investment companies know one simple truth: if they want to keep their existing customers, they need to prevent them from transferring their money to a rival investment firm - by producing high returns for them.

As long as interest rates are low and there is no financial crisis looming in the near future, investing in risky assets is almost the only way to "stay in the game". Therefore, interest rate levels and their fluctuations are very important to your investment portfolio.

Practical Conclusions

The indicators presented here all have a common denominator: they must be analyzed over a period time, so the direction of their trend is revealed. When you analyze them over time, it is particularly important to check how an increase or decrease in specific indicators impacts inflationary pressures and hence causes an increase or decrease in interest rates. This information can be used as a powerful tool for the optimal management of your investment portfolio.

Epilogue

REMEMBER:

**You won't get any prizes just for knowing things
you'll only be rewarded for your actions.
You gained valuable information:
Use it!**

Has this book helped you better understand
and manage your finances?
Please let me know - post an Amazon review.
Much appreciated,
Jacob Nayman

49449475R00084

Made in the USA
Middletown, DE
16 October 2017